# PRIMATES

# CONTENTS

| | |
|---|---|
| The planet of the apes | 4–5 |
| Mother, father, and children | 6–7 |
| Social life | 8–9 |
| Prosimians | 10–11 |
| Night vision | 12–13 |
| Noses | 14–15 |
| Tails | 16–17 |
| The colobus and the langur | 18–19 |
| Macaques and other monkeys | 20–21 |
| Tailless acrobats | 22–23 |
| The orangutan | 24–25 |
| The clever chimpanzee | 26–27 |
| The mighty gorilla | 28–29 |
| | |
| Glossary | 30 |
| Index | 31 |

## GENERAL CLASSIFICATION OF PRIMATES

| PROSIMIANS | | Lemuroids: lemurs |
|---|---|---|
| | | Indrids: indris and sirakas |
| | | Daubentoniidae: aye-ayes |
| | | Lorisids: galagos, loris, potos |
| | | Tarsidiidae: tarsiers |
| SIMIANS | Platyrrhinians: | Callithricidae: titis and tamarins |
| | | Cebidae: squirrel monkeys, spider monkeys, capuchins, howler monkeys, marcaris, night monkeys, sakis, woolly spider monkeys |
| | Catarrhinians: | Colobinae: colobus, langurs |
| | | Cercopithecoids: macaques, baboons, geladas, cercopithecus |
| HOMINOIDS | | Hylobates: siamangs, gibbons |
| | | Pongidae: orangutans, chimpanzees, gorillas |
| | | Hominids: humans |

Original title of book in Spanish:
El Fascinante Mundo de... Los Primates
© Parramón Ediciones, S.A.
Published by Parramón Ediciones, S.A.

Author: Maria Ángels Julivert
Illustrations: Marcel Socías Studios

English text © Copyright 1996 by Barron's Educational Series, Inc.

*All inquiries should be addressed to:*
Barron's Educational Series, Inc.
250 Wireless Boulevard
Hauppauge, NY 11788-3917

ISBN: 0-8120-9755-6

Library of Congress Catalog Card No. 96-13225

**Library of Congress Cataloging-in-Publication Data**

Julivert, Maria Ángels.
  [Fascinante mundo de— los primates. English]
  The fascinating world of— primates / by Maria Ángels Julivert ; illustrations by Marcel Socías Studios.
      p.  cm.
  Includes index.
  Summary: Describes the physical characteristics, habits, and habitat of such five-toed, five-fingered primates as the gorilla, chimpanzee, and orangutan.
  ISBN 0-8120-9755-6
  1. Primates—Juvenile literature. [1. Primates.] I. Marcel Socías Studios.  II. Title.
QL737.P9J8513   1996
599.8—dc20                                          96-13225
                                                    CIP
                                                    AC

Printed in Spain
9 8 7 6 5 4 3 2 1

# THE FASCINATING WORLD OF...

# PRIMATES

by
Maria Ángels Julivert

Illustrations by Marcel Socías Studios

BARRON'S

# THE PLANET OF THE APES

The order of primates includes a large number of different-sized animals of diverse appearances and lifestyles, from the pygmy titi or the galago dwarf, which weighs less than 3.5 ounces (100 grams), to the mighty gorilla, which weighs more than 440 pounds (200 kilograms). It should not be forgotten that we humans also belong to this order.

Primates have five fingers and five toes with a nail at the end of each one. In most species of primates, the thumb opposes, or touches, the other fingers, enabling apes to pick up objects. Primates may have a long or a short tail, and some, such as the chimpanzee, have no tail whatsoever. Certain species, like the spider money, possess a prehensile, or grabbing, tail. The gibbon walks upright, but most primates move around on all four limbs. Most primates are arboreal, that is to say they are tree-dwelling animals, although some, such as the baboon, live on the ground.

Primates are divided into two large groups: prosimians and simians or anthropoids. The former are the most primitive and include lemurs, galagos, lorises, and tarsiers; the latter comprise so-called monkeys (such as titis, tamarins, squirrel monkeys, macaques, baboons, mandrills, and so on) and gibbons, chimpanzees, orangutans, gorillas, and humans.

*Above:* The pygmy titi measures less than 8 inches (20 centimeters) from its head to the tip of its tail, while a male gorilla can be more than 6 feet (1.90 meters) tall.

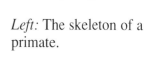

*Right:* Japanese macaque with its young.

*Left:* The skeleton of a primate.

*Below:* The shapes of the hands and feet of primates vary according to the lifestyle of each animal.

CHIMPANZEE  GIBBON  AYE-AYE

# MOTHER, FATHER, AND CHILDREN

Although it is common for certain species to give birth to twins, most female primates tend to give birth to one offspring at a time. During the first stage of the baby primate's life, it is breast-fed by its mother. The offspring rides on its mother's back by clinging to her hair. Normally the mother rears her baby by herself. In certain primate societies, such as that of the baboon, this task is shared by several females. On occasion, the males also cooperate in bringing up the young; such is the case of the titi, a small day-hunting monkey.

During infancy, young simians learn to behave by observing and imitating their mothers and the rest of the mem-

FEMALE BABOON
FEEDING HER YOUNG

bers of the group. The more advanced on the evolutionary scale a species is, the longer the young remain at their parents' sides. For instance, the lemur (a prosimian) can already take care of itself a few months after birth. On the other hand, the young chimpanzee and gorilla can remain for more than five years with their parents.

Young males tend to abandon the group while the females stay on. In certain species, it is the young female who leaves the group to join another group. In other species, both the males and the females are forced out of the group when they come of age.

*Right:* The young of the common lemur have a baby-sitter to watch them.

*Bottom left and above:* The babies are breast-fed by their mother and remain firmly attached to her for months.

*Bottom right:* Often, there are observable differences between males and females. In the illustration, a male and female howler monkey.

FEMALE TOTA CARRYING HER YOUNG

# SOCIAL LIFE

Primates are social animals. They live in groups whose size and makeup vary greatly. There are groups of as few as five members to bands of over a hundred individuals. Many primates (such as the macaque or the olive-green Anubus baboon) live in groups made up of several adult males and females and their young.

There is a wide variety of parental and territorial relationships. In most cases, there also exists divisions, or rankings, among the males. The same may occur in the relationships among the females.

Some species of primates form harems in which there is a single dominant male and several females and their young. This is the case of the gorilla. The gelada and the hamadryas baboons combine several groups of different harems to form a clan, only expelling males that cannot reproduce, and forming communities of more than 150 individuals.

Other simians (like the gibbon, the indri, and the titi) live in family groups consisting of a male and a female and their young.

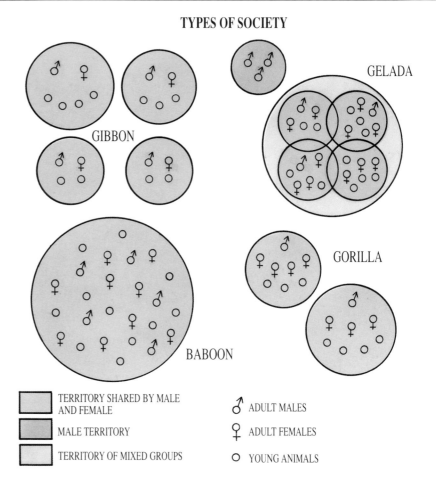

## TYPES OF SOCIETY

GIBBON

GELADA

BABOON

GORILLA

TERRITORY SHARED BY MALE AND FEMALE

MALE TERRITORY

TERRITORY OF MIXED GROUPS

♂ ADULT MALES

♀ ADULT FEMALES

○ YOUNG ANIMALS

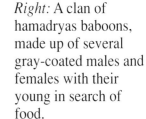

*Right:* A clan of hamadryas baboons, made up of several gray-coated males and females with their young in search of food.

*Left:* A female olive-green Anubus baboon shows her fear of the dominant female by grimacing, lifting up her hind leg, and raising her tail to a vertical position.

# PROSIMIANS

Prosimians are the least evolved primates. Lemurs, indris, sirakas, aye-ayes, galagos, lorises, and potos belong to this group. They have flat fingernails and toenails except for the nail on the second toe of each foot, which is a claw. These species of prosimians live in the jungles and forests of Madagascar, Africa, India, Myanmar, Indonesia, and the Philippines.

The largest family is that of the lemuroids, which lives on the island of Madagascar and feeds on fruit, leaves, flowers, and, very occasionally, insects. Although some are nocturnal (such as the lemur mouse or the lemur dwarf), the larger ones are diurnal (like the ring-tailed lemur and the jumper lemur). The arms of these thick-coated, tree-dwelling animals are shorter than their legs and they have a long tail that, on occasion, is longer than the rest of the body.

The indris and sirakas are native to Madagascar and are larger than the lemurs. The common indri is the largest prosimian of them all; with its short tail it is capable of jumping up to 33 feet (10 meters) from one tree to another.

Little is known about the aye-aye, an unusual nocturnal prosimian from northern Madagascar that is currently on the verge of extinction, or disappearing forever. It has large teeth and enormous eyes. Its fingers are long and it has claws, except for the big toe of each foot, which has a flat toenail. Its

BLACK LEMUR

extraordinarily long index finger is used for extracting pulp from fruit and larvae from holes and cracks in the tree trunks.

AYE-AYE

SIRAKA

*Right:* The ring-tailed lemur uses its long tail, filled with a strong odor, as a warning signal against possible rivals.

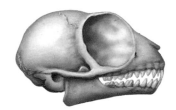

TARSIER

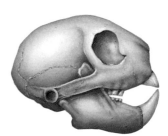

AYE-AYE

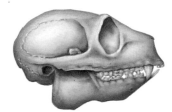

INDRI

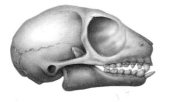

GALAGO

# NIGHT VISION

Galagos, lorises, and potos are night-hunting creatures with very developed sight and hearing. These tree-dwelling animals feed on insects and fruit. Instead of a toenail, the second toe has a claw, which is used for cleaning.

Galagos, which live in Africa, move quickly and easily. When jumping from tree to tree, they use their tail to help them balance. Their acute sense of hearing helps them to locate prey, mostly insects, although they are also very fond of resin, or natural gum from trees.

The Asian loris and the African poto are skilled climbers, although they move slowly and carefully. They often remain motionless for hours and have a very developed sense of smell to detect prey (caterpillars, flies, butterflies). They mark their territory by urinating in different places to leave their own strong odor, or scent.

The tarsier is part of a suborder that is independent from prosimians and simians. There are currently three surviving species in the jungles of Southeast Asia. The tarsier is a night-hunting creature with an acute sense of hearing. It is an excellent climber and jumper. This animal has many special identifying marks, like the claw on the third toe, long hind legs, and a long hairless tail that ends in a tuft.

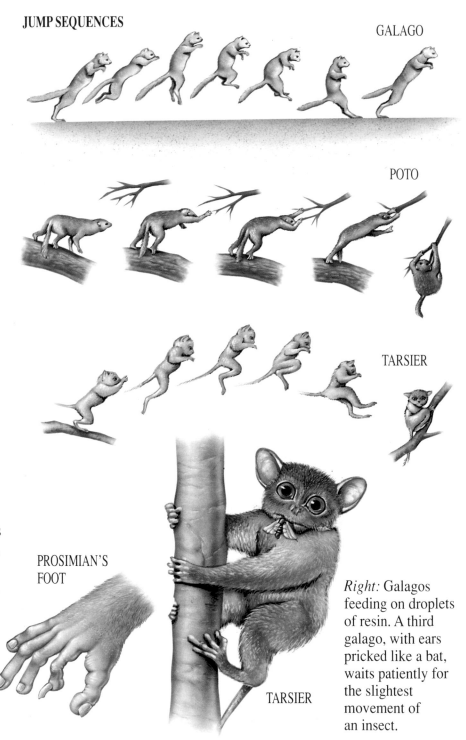

JUMP SEQUENCES

GALAGO

POTO

TARSIER

PROSIMIAN'S FOOT

TARSIER

*Right:* Galagos feeding on droplets of resin. A third galago, with ears pricked like a bat, waits patiently for the slightest movement of an insect.

# NOSES

Simians are divided into two main groups: the platyrrhinians and the catarrhinians. The first group are native to Central and South America. They have a broad, flat nose, with widely separated nostrils. The second group, the catarrhinians, live in Africa and Asia. Their nose is thinner, with the nostrils closer together and facing downward. Their name derives from the Latin word for nose, *rhinos*.

There are two families of platyrrhinians: the callithricidae (titis and tamarins) and the cebidae (squirrel monkeys and spider monkeys).

Both the titi and the tamarin are small day-hunting simians. They live in trees and feed on fruit, flowers, and nectar, or tiny animals like insects and snails. The platyrrhinians are the only simians to possess claws on all of their fingers and toes except for the largest toe, which has a flat toenail. They have a colorful, soft coat and have large mustaches, manes, or tufts of hair around the ears. These monkeys generally live in a group of a male, a female, and the offspring. The size of this group is between four and fifteen. The territory occupied by each family varies greatly and the size is determined by the quantity of food required for their needs.

*Right:* The imposing mustache of an Emperor tamarin seated in his tree-top world.

GOLDEN LION TAMARIN

TITI WITH WHITE TUFTS

COTTONY TAMARIN

GOELDI TAMARIN

CATARRHINIAN

PLATYRRHINIAN

# TAILS

The most numerous family of platyrrhinian simians is that of the cebidae. This family is made up of various species including: the long-armed spider monkey, the agile and minute squirrel spider, the graceful capuchin, the noisy howler monkey, and the strange-looking uakari. With the exception of the uakari, these primates have a long tail that is prehensile, or used for wrapping around objects, in certain species (such as the spider monkey and the howler monkey) and is used for clinging on to tree branches. Some species (like the capuchin), live in groups made up of a male and several females, and others (like the night monkey), have the same partner for life.

The howler monkey makes a howling noise, heard over great distances. This sound helps it locate other groups.

The uakari's head, with its hairless face and high forehead, gives this

RED UAKARI

monkey an unusual appearance. This short-tailed creature is a daytime animal.

The night monkey is the only nocturnal monkey of the entire family. It has enormous eyes and, during the day, it sleeps hidden in the vegetation or in a hole in a tree trunk. It lives on fruit, leaves, nectar, insects, and certain small birds. The night monkey, unlike the spider monkey, does not have a prehensile tail.

The spider monkey, with its long arms and impressive tail, used both for swinging through the trees and for picking up objects, is a magnificent tree-dwelling ape whose territory takes up large stretches of forest.

*Right:* Excluding the tail, the squirrel monkey only measures 11.5 inches (30 centimeters) in length. It moves with speed and great balance in its tree kingdom. The squirrel monkey lives in groups of 30 to 40 males and females. The female takes care of the young and, during the mating season, the males fight each other for a partner.

SPIDER MONKEY

FAMILY OF NIGHT MONKEYS

HOWLER MONKEY

# THE COLOBUS AND THE LANGUR

*Below:* The western rusty-colored colobus lives in the forests and savannas of Gambia and Senegal.

Catarrhinian simians are divided into two large groups: hominoids (hylobates, pongidae, and hominoids) and cercopithecoids. This last family of monkeys is very numerous. They can be easily recognized because their buttocks have several noticeable rough spots. They are divided into two subfamilies: the colobinae (which include the colobus and the langur) and the cercopithecoid (which comprise the remainder, such as baboons and the cercopithecidae). The colobinae are noted for their thin body, long nonprehensile tail, and tiny or nonexistent thumbs.

The langur inhabits the jungles and forests of Asia. Generally they spend most of their time aboveground in tree-tops. They feed on leaves, but also eat fruits, flowers, and seeds. The common langur is regarded as a sacred animal in India, and it is not unusual to see it in populated areas. This graceful gray-haired (except around its eyes, ears, hands, and feet) creature lives in groups ranging from six to seventy individuals. Males do not take care of the young.

The colobus (the African relative of the langur) lives in the mountains and jungles. It has no thumbs, and feeds almost exclusively on leaves.

*Above:* The males of the big-nosed monkey of Borneo have such an enormous nose that it hangs over their mouth. Little is known about this curious animal.

*Right:* An uninvited male langur being fought off.

*Right:* The colobus guereza, an excellent acrobat, has been hunted for its fine, beautiful coat. At present it is a protected species.

# MACAQUES AND OTHER MONKEYS

Cercopithecoids, which includes most monkeys seen in zoos, are found throughout Africa and Asia. They have adapted to many different environments, from tropical rain forests, to mountaintops (such as the Himalayas), to the savanna, or dry, treeless plains. They have long, thick hair and, in certain species, bright-colored markings on the face and other parts of their bodies. The canine, or dog-like, teeth of the male are much longer than the rest of the teeth. They have a type of pouch in their cheeks for carrying food to a safe place. These animals prefer fruit, but they will normally eat just about anything: seeds, flowers, roots, insects, crabs, birds, and small mammals.

The macaque, a brown-haired monkey with a hairless face that is occasionally red in color, lives in Asia. It is a social animal, living in large groups of adult males and females.

The baboon, an African monkey, also lives in large groups. These groups join together in packs to hunt. Their long snout and very developed canine teeth give them a frightening appearance. The majority of these species are made up of drills and mandrills.

The hamadryas baboon has brown hair and a mantle of long, gray hair about the head. It lives in groups made up of a male and several females with their young.

*Above:* A Japanese macaque washes sweet potatoes to remove the sand.

*Right:* For baboons, grooming is done for cleanliness and as a social activity to bring different members of the group together.

MANDRILL

MALE TOTA

CERCOPITENECUS DIANA

# TAILLESS ACROBATS

I n addition to humans (hominid), the main order of primates (hominidae superfamily) is made up of two other families: the hylobates (the siamang and the gibbon) and our closest ancestors, the pongidae (the orangutan, the chimpanzee, and the gorilla).

Both families have large brains. It is much more developed than those of all other animals (with the exception of humans). These animals are all tailless, and their arms are longer than their legs. With the exception of the gorilla, which lives for the most part on solid ground, most of these animals spend practically their entire life aboveground in trees.

Hylobates, which are smaller than pongidae, are found in the jungles of Southeast Asia and the Malay peninsula. They live in small family groups consisting of a male, a female, and their offspring. The females give birth to a single baby at a time. These tree-dwelling creatures swing from branch to branch with amazing agility. The gibbon, of which there are several different species, is easily recognized by the color of its hair and the markings on its face. Gibbons are known for being great acrobats. The siamang is somewhat larger and slower than the gibbon. It has long black hair, and it has a highly developed laryngeal sac, a kind of voice box, that is inflated to produce powerful screeches.

SIAMANG

BRACHIATION

GIBBON

*Left:* The sac on its neck helps the siamang make many different kinds of screeches and howls.

*Right and below:* The gibbon's ability to swing from one branch to another is known as *brachiation.*

*Left:* When the gibbon yells, it shows its fangs to frighten its enemies.

# THE ORANGUTAN

The orangutan, the chimpanzee, and the gorilla belong to the family of pongidae. The orangutan, a red-haired ape, is found only in the forests of Sumatra and Borneo. It has long arms. With the exception of its face, its body is covered with long red hair. The adult male is larger and heavier than the female, and the older males develop fatty flab on either side of their face, giving them a funny appearance.

The orangutan spends almost its entire life in the treetops and rarely descends to the forest floor. It builds large nests, using branches and leaves, in the highest treetops and feeds upon fruit (nuts, litchis, mangoes, figs), leaves, shoots, flowers, and seeds. The orangutan often adds insects, bird's eggs, and chicks to its vegetarian diet.

The orangutan likes to stay by itself. Once a year though, during the mating season, it takes a mate. During this period, the male tries to approach as many females as possible and, when successful, fights off any competing males.

After almost nine months of gestation, or carrying a baby in her stomach, the female orangutan gives birth to a single offspring (occasionally apes give birth to twins) that she will breast-feed for three years. During this time, she will not have any more children. Young orangutans remain in the care of their mothers until they are seven or eight years old. Because of the increased destruction of its jungle home, the orangutan is in danger of extinction. To help save this very intelligent animal, orangutans are now a protected species.

*Above:* The accumulation of fatty folds on its face and under its throat gives this old male orangutan a funny appearance.

*Right:* Clinging to the branches with their long arms and prehensile, or gripping, feet, orangutans search for their favorite food, fruit.

*Left:* A female orangutan kissing her child.

# THE CLEVER CHIMPANZEE

The chimpanzee lives in the forests, jungles, and savannas, or dry treeless plains, of Africa. Like the orangutan and the gorilla, the chimpanzee belongs to the family of pongidae. Its arms are longer than its legs. It has big ears and a highly developed sense of smell and hearing. It feeds mainly on vegetables (fruit, seeds, and leaves), although sometimes it will eat tiny animals, especially insects. Chimpanzees live in mixed groups of males and females, sometimes in large numbers; but there also exist groups of single males or females with their offspring. The young remain at their mother's side from five to seven years.

Scientific experiments have indicated that the chimpanzee is a very intelligent creature. They are very curious animals. They manufacture tools for use in everyday life, such as sticks for trapping termites and ants. The chimpanzee defends itself by hitting its enemy with a stick or by throwing stones at it. For a bed, the chimpanzee builds a nest with leaves and branches from the treetops.

The most highly developed and varied of all simians, the chimpanzee can make many gestures and sounds (howls, screeches, grunts). Chimpanzees also use many different facial expressions for communicating with other chimpanzees.

*Above:* In addition to the common chimpanzee, there is also the pygmy chimpanzee, or bonobo, that is native to the jungles of Zaire.

*Right:* The chimpanzee makes tools for performing certain tasks. This stick is ideal for catching termites.

*Left:* A chimpanzee resting in the branch of a tree.

*Below:* Some chimpanzee facial expressions.

PLAYFUL

ASKING FOR FOOD

AGGRESSIVE

FEARFUL

SUBMISSIVE

FEARFUL OF STRONGER CHIMPANZEE

# THE MIGHTY GORILLA

The mighty gorilla, the largest primate of all, lives in the tropical forests of central Africa. This ape has blackish hair, a large head, small eyes, and a wide, flattened nose. An adult male can weigh as much as 440 pounds (200 kilograms). Females are smaller. Unlike young gorillas, adult males have a streak of silver hair down their back.

The gorilla lives in stable, or lasting, groups, of between five and thirty members. Groups have one dominant adult male, or leader, several females with their young, and various young males. The male with the silver streak down its back is the leader, and it is his task to protect the group. Female gorillas give birth to one offspring every four years. When they reach adulthood, young males abandon the group to form their own groups. Female gorillas change groups when they are old enough to have babies.

Gorillas are active during the day and spend most of their time on the ground. They walk on all fours, placing their knuckles on the ground to move around. Gorillas are chiefly vegetarian, feeding on leaves, shoots, roots, and fruit.

The destruction of forests and hunting have put the gorilla in danger of extinction, especially the mountain gorilla, a magnificent animal very much like humans.

*Right:* Gorillas live in groups. The dominant male is easy to recognize by his size and the silver streak of hair running down his back.

*Left: Copito de Nieve* (Snowflake), the only known living albino, or white, gorilla, lives in the Barcelona Zoo.

*Below:* To protect themselves from the sun, gorillas use large leaves as a kind of hat.

# GLOSSARY

**Agile:** Ability to move quickly with balance and coordination.

**Albino:** Animal lacking pigmentation in the hair, eyes, and skin.

**Arboreal:** Living in the trees.

**Brachiation:** The action of moving from one branch to another using the arms.

**Gestation:** Pregnancy.

**Habitat:** The physical environment where an animal lives.

**Harem:** Group of females that live with one single male.

**Hierarchy:** Order or rank within a group.

**Prehensile:** Tail or limb adapted for seizing, grasping, or taking hold of something.

**Pulp:** The soft part inside fruit.

**Rival:** One that competes with another by fighting in order to obtain a single objective.

**Simian:** Related to or resembling apes or monkeys.

**Species:** Group of animals or plants that have a series of common characteristics by which they can be grouped together and distinguished from other species.

**Territoriality:** The behavior of an animal defending its territory.

# INDEX

acrobat, 18, 22
anthropoids, 4
aye-aye, 10

baboon, 20
big-nosed monkey, 18
bonobo, 26
brachiation, 22

callithricidae, 14
callosities, 18
canine teeth, 20
capuchin, 16
catarrhinian, 14, 18
cebidae, 14, 16
cercopitenecus diana, 20
cercopithecoids, 18, 20
chimpanzee, 4, 6, 22, 24, 26
clan, 8
claw, 10, 12, 14
colobinae, 18
colobus, 18
colobus guereza, 18
cottony tamarin, 14

deforestation, 28
drills, 20

emperor tamarin, 14
extinction, 10, 24, 28

facial expressions, 26
fangs, 22
fatty flab, 24
fingernails, 10, 14

galago, 4, 10, 12
gelada, 8
gestures, 26
gibbon, 4, 8, 22
Goeldi tamarin, 14
Golden lion tamarin, 14
gorilla, 4, 6, 8, 22, 24, 26, 28
grooming, 20

hamadryas baboon, 8, 20
harem, 8
hierarchies, 20
hominoids, 18, 22
howler monkey, 6, 16
howling, howls, 16, 22
humans, 4, 22
hylobates, 18, 22

indri, 8, 10

Japanese macaque, 4, 20
jumper lemur, 10

knuckles, 28

langur, 6, 18
laryngeal sac, 22
lemur, 4, 6, 10,
lemur dwarf, 10
lemur mouse, 10
lemuroids, 10
loris, 4, 10, 12

macaque, 4, 8, 18, 20
mandrill, 4, 20
mantle, 20
mountain gorilla, 28

night monkcy, 16

offspring, 6, 8, 14, 16, 18, 20, 22, 28
olive-green Anubus baboon, 8
orangutan, 4, 22, 24, 26

platyrrhinians, 14, 16
pongidae, 18, 22, 24, 26

potos, 10, 12
prehensile tail, 4, 16
primate, 4, 6, 8, 10, 22, 28
prosimian, 4, 6, 10, 12
pygmy chimpanzee, 26

ranking, 8
resin, 12
ring-tailed lemur, 10

scent, 12
siamang, 22
simian, 4, 6, 12, 14, 16, 18, 24
siraka, 10
spider monkey, 4, 14, 16
squirrel monkey, 4, 14, 16

tamarin, 4, 14
tarsier, 4, 12
territory, 8, 14, 16, 24
thumb, 4, 18
titi, 4, 6, 8, 12, 14
titi with white tufts, 14
toenails, 10, 14
tota, 20
tree-dwelling, 4, 10, 12, 16, 22

uakari, 16